The Ayterzedd

The Ayterzedd

A Bestiary of (mostly) Alien Beings by Brian Allgar

Kelsay Books

© 2018 Brian Allgar. All rights reserved. This material may not be reproduced in any form, published, reprinted, recorded, performed, broadcast, rewritten or redistributed without the explicit permission of Brian Allgar. All such actions are strictly prohibited by law.

Cover design: Sylvia Fairley

Cover photograph: 'A Circular Library' (photographer unknown)

ISBN: 978-1-947465-43-5

Kelsay Books
Aldrich Press
www.kelsaybooks.com

Special thanks to Sylvia Fairley
for putting the Ayterzedd in his library

Acknowledgments

The following pieces have appeared in the publications or online poetry magazines shown.

The Spectator: "The Millibrand"
Lighten Up Online: "The Farfeloo," "The Hurkle," "The Ombery," "The Quembling," "The Trilph," "The Yucketeer," and "The Xenolith"
Snakeskin: "The Blathersnick"

Contents

Prelude	11
The Ayterzedd	12
The Blathersnick	14
The Crimp	15
The Drangler	16
The Easter Bunny	17
The Farfeloo	18
The Gloopum	19
The Hurkle	20
Interlude	21
The Jibblish	22
The Krayders	23
The Luberos	25
The Millibrand	26
The Nerbivore	27
The Ombery	28
The Pigglejay	29
The Quembling	30
The Rumpkin	31
The Snidgit	33
The Trilph	34
The Urbloid	36
The Vegetable Feast	37
The Wapsicles	38
The Xenolith	39
The Yucketeer	41
The Zoff	42
Postlude	43

About the Author

Prelude

What's that you say? The Pigglejay?
It doesn't ring a bell.
No doubt it's from some silly tale
Your mother likes to tell.

Why she must fill your head with stuff
Like that, I've no idea.
Such feeble intellectual fluff
Will ruin your career.

But though I'm sure there's no such thing,
Let's carry out some tests.
We'll put it to a know-it-all
Who loves receiving guests.

Like that, we'll knock these fantasies
Completely from your head.
So let us go and see him now;
He's called—

The Ayterzedd

The Ayterzedd, though very small,
Knows everything worth knowing.
Just ask him, and he'll tell you all,
His little eyestalks glowing.

His learning is a mystery;
He never went to college,
And yet his brain seems to contain
Encyclopaedic knowledge

From Alien Biology
(That's folk from other planets),
He'll take you to Zoology
(Gorillas, groupers, gannets).

But please be warned: each question is
The catalyst that triggers
An endless speech; he can't select
Specific facts and figures.

Once he's begun, his speech will run
From Blathersnick to Zoff,
So do not—Wait! Oh, no! Too late!
I fear you've set him off.

****

"Good morning, what a lovely day!
How kind of you to visit.
You ask about the Pigglejay?
Now, what the devil is it?

I'm pretty sure I knew before
My whiskers started thinning.
Well, never mind; it's best, I find,
To start at the beginning.

A rather lengthy process, yet
It's quite a useful trick.
I'll have to scan the alphabet,
So first—"

The Blathersnick

The Blathersnick will make you sick;
His habits are disgusting.
He offers toys to girls and boys,
So innocent and trusting.

He takes them off for little walks
Beside the murky river,
And on the way, he talks and talks—
His voice would make you shiver.

He tells them tales of whelks and whales
Who swim upon the torrent,
But all the time, he plans a crime
That's utterly abhorrent.

He slyly chats of brindled cats,
Of creatures strange and creepy.
The sun has gone; he blathers on
Until they're feeling sleepy.

And when he's got them far from town
He stuffs their mouths with honey,
Then, whoosh! he shakes them upside-down
To snitch their pocket-money.

The Crimp

The Crimp's an immaculate fellow
With manners polite and refined.
His gaiters are buttercup-yellow,
His boots always polished and shined.

His clothes are the latest in fashion;
He's someone the tailors adore,
And Liberty ties are his passion;
He has seven dozen, or more.

He never wears belts, only braces;
He's elegant, supple and thin,
So nimble and neat, and so light on his feet
He can dance on the head of a pin.

His taste is impeccably highbrow,
The stern philosophical type,
And he'll show by the lift of an eyebrow
That he thinks what you're reading is tripe.

But although he's the soul of discretion—
His face, when he's shocked, barely twitches—
He's an excellent guest, with a quip or a jest
That can have the whole party in stitches.

There is only one thing that disgraces
This paragon, one little sin:
It's his voice, the most raucous of basses—
When he sings, it's an ear-splitting din.

The Drangler

The Drangler creeps about at night
To do his dirty deeds
And slake his gruesome appetite,
His cravings and his needs.
He picks a spot beyond the light,
Well-hidden in the weeds,
And when he's sure he's out of sight,
He gluttonously feeds
On snails and slugs, on beetles, bugs,
On worms and centipedes.

But if his mother catches him,
She rages fit to burst:
"I've told you time and time again—
You have to rinse them first!"

Although it's not an alien,
I find it rather funny,
So here's a little anecdote
About—

The Easter Bunny

He told his baker what he wanted,
Paid him lots of money—
A loaf of bread with paws and head
Shaped like an Easter bunny.

That Sunday, he collected it,
A bunny to the life
With golden crust and floury dust,
And gave it to his wife.

"So realistic!" she exclaimed,
"With ears so long and floppy,
Its fluffy tail so soft and pale—
I think I'll call it 'Hoppy'"

But when she set it on a plate,
The crust began to crack,
And uncooked dough began to flow,
Revealing hints of black.

Disintegration was complete;
The thing began to waddle.
Their baker friend, to serve his end,
Had used a living model!

The rabbit quivered with alarm
That sunny Easter morn,
Then bolted for the open door
And pooped upon the lawn.

The Farfeloo

The Farfeloo lives in a rickety shack
With a roof that lets in all the rain,
So he washes his clothes while they're still on his back,
And the neighbours believe he's insane,

For he dries them by leaping to twice his own height
Till he's puffing and panting and pink,
But sometimes his trousers seem awfully tight,
And he wonders if rain makes them shrink.

He eats very little, and drinks his own spittle,
Eked out by a diet of worms,
Preferring them young, for they tickle his tongue
As each annelid wriggles and squirms.

He keeps an umbrella to hand in the cellar
In case it should rain underground,
For there is his treasure, a pearl beyond measure,
Which has to be kept safe and sound.

He takes it down nightly, and locks it up tightly,
Then padlocks the door with a chain.
If burglars came calling, it would be appalling
To lose his detachable brain.

The Gloopum

The Gloopum, I regret to say,
Is not a pretty fellow;
His hair is lank, his breath is dank,
His teeth are mustard-yellow.

His lumpy hands are blotched and scarred
With pustular infections,
His eyes strabismic, staring hard
In different directions.

On meeting him, you'd think him vile,
Unwashed, unkempt and smelly,
And if you saw his horrid smile,
Your knees would turn to jelly.

Yet inwardly, he's gentle, kind,
An aesthete in his fashion;
He'll write an ode, befriend a toad,
And roses are his passion.

His days are spent in pure delight,
Poetically dreaming.
But *never* think of him at night,
Or else you'll wake up screaming.

The Hurkle

*The first line of this poem is borrowed from the title of a story
by Theodore Sturgeon*

The Hurkle is a happy beast
Who strikes endearing poses.
He has three heads, a dozen eyes,
And six assorted noses.

His furry tongue is five feet long,
The colour of tobacco,
But when it's stretched, can almost reach
The constellation Draco.

He's fond of children, adults too,
And sings to them divinely.
He helps old ladies cross the street
And pats their heads benignly;

His dress is somewhat dandyish,
Bewigged, befrocked and bodiced;
His eating habits usually
Are admirably modest.

But after dieting for Lent,
Grown ravenously thinner,
He'll gladly munch your kids for lunch,
And gobble you for dinner.

A note about the Hurkle's tongue:

Normally, when at rest, it is about five feet long. But its almost infinite elasticity has enabled the Hurkles to devise a very effective form of interstellar travel. Having identified a likely planet, a Hurkle shoots out its tongue and anchors it to a solid object like a rock or tree on the chosen planet. Then, simply by contracting the muscles of its tongue, the Hurkle's body is whisked through space to rejoin the pioneering organ. That is how there came to be so many Hurkles on the Earth.

Interlude

The Ayterzedd was growing hoarse;
His mouth and throat were dry.
He stopped to drink a glass of beer
And eat a slice of pie.
(I noticed, when he spoke again,
He'd skipped the letter 'I'.)

The Jibblish

The Jibblish loves to take a book
And turn it upside-down,
Then read it back to front, although
It causes him to frown.

The plot is difficult to grasp;
It's crowded with events
That finish long before they start,
And really make no sense.

Before they've even left the house,
The travellers arrive,
And corpses buried in the wood
Turn out to be alive.

The stumps are drawn, the teams go home,
Then play a game of cricket.
The captain wins the lottery
Before he's bought the ticket.

The hero and the heroine
Are man and wife, and yet
How could the pair be married, when
They've never even met?

Or what about the teacher who
Will later go to school?
The Jibblish wonders if the author
Takes him for a fool.

It seems implausible and strained;
By now, his head is spinning.
But finally it's all explained—
The end is the beginning.

The Krayders

On a planet of Alpha Centauri,
The twentieth world from the sun,
They tell a remarkable story
Of how independence was won.

From space came a war fleet of Krayders
With armour that nothing could pierce,
An onslaught of cruel invaders,
Belligerent, brutal and fierce.

The Alphans were easily beaten
By conquerors dark and depraved.
Resisters were roasted and eaten,
The rest of the planet enslaved.

But one of them laughed at enslavement;
Defying her masters and lords,
She brazenly walked on the pavement
Reserved for the swaggering hordes.

She fearlessly held her position
As Krayders moved in to attack,
And knowing their deep superstition,
She planted her feet on a crack.

They gasped in amazement, and bleated
"Behold what she does, and survives!"
They fell to their knees, and entreated
This Legend to spare them their lives.

Today, they are sheepishly working
As waiters in bars and cafés,
Obsequious, smiling and smirking
While counting the tips on their trays.

The Krayders are sometimes resentful,
But know there is no going back,
For they tremble with awe at the day that they saw
The Goddess who stepped on a crack.

The Luberos

They say the Luberos is vile,
Venereal and vicious,
And gives a meaning to the words
'Licentious' and 'lubricious'.

They say that of the seven sins,
His favourite is Lust.
"Let's gather rosebuds", he exclaims,
"Before we come to dust!"

They say he's thoroughly depraved,
His habits are pernicious,
And when he sees a pretty girl,
He murmurs "How delicious!"

They say he haunts the seaside towns
And wanders on the beaches,
Devouring with salacious eyes
Those little golden peaches.

They say the the Luberos is bent
On foul debauchery ...
Yet all he really wants to do
Is take them home for tea.

The Millibrand

Midwinter, and the gringeing Ghoves
Did quave and quemble on the ice,
The Cameroon howled like a loon
And nibbled frozen lice.

"The Millibrand is close at hand!"
He sneezed with fear and snarled with pain.
"A thousand legs like stumpy pegs,
Yet only half a brain!

He'll have our lives, he'll eat our wives!
He'll slurp us up and crunch our bones!"
They heard him sniff—he'd caught their whiff—
They heard his hungry moans.

He snuffed and snurtled, whuffed and whurtled,
Thumped and crumped; his frenzied drumming
Shook the ground with every bound.
The Millibrand was coming!

They called for help, they called for kelp,
They even called upon the Loris,
But he, extinct, just blurped and blinked,
And mumbled: "Try the Borriss."

Though limp and lame, the hero came,
And chorkled through the snigid forest.
The Millibrand made one last stand,
But ended bagged and borrissed.

The Nerbivore

Subsisting, as his name suggests,
Exclusively on Nerbs,
He lures them from their cosy nests
And sprinkles them with herbs.

He chops them with a well-honed blade
And brings them to the boil,
Then steeps them in a marinade
Of lemon juice and oil.

He sets aside the juicy eyes,
So tender and so sweet,
And eats them with ecstatic cries,
His special little treat.

   *****

At least, that's what he used to do
Before he came to Earth.
But here, the Nerbs are very few—
In fact, an utter dearth.

It seemed as though the Nerbivore
Would soon become extinct:
Deprived of food, he'd be no more ...
But Nature kindly winked.

He found a creature that he bastes;
The flavour is superb.
When lightly barbecued, it tastes
Exactly like a Nerb.

But please be warned: he hunts at night,
And swoops down like a bat,
So never let her out of sight,
Your precious Persian cat.

The Ombery

The Ombery dwells in a cave on the moon,
On the dark side that nobody sees.
He's the oddest of creatures, a mixture of features
Supported by knees like a bee's,

With the ears of a cat and the wings of a bat
And the intricate eyes of a spider,
The crest of a cock, and the jaws of a croc,
But much toothier, smilier, wider.

"Time for lunch!" he declares, for he constantly wears
His heart on his sleeve like a clock,
So he knows to the second the time of his life
From the sound of the tick and the tock.

He has to stick tight to perpetual night,
For the sunshine would turn him to powder;
He lives, as he must, on a diet of dust
And occasional arthropod chowder.

He carries a spoon as he strolls on the moon
To scoop out the brains of a friend
Who is happy to give him a piece of his mind,
For the Omberies borrow and lend.

The following day he will gladly repay,
And with interest, the whole of the loan.
"Reimbursement in kind" is the contract they signed,
So he'll throw in a mind of his own.

The Pigglejay

And so we come to Pigglejays—
It wouldn't do to miss one!
They have their funny little ways,
And none more so than this one.

Oh, how the creature yearned to fly!
The effort drove her frantic.
Her wings, alas, were minuscule,
Her body was gigantic.

She flapped and flapped, but only made
A feeble whirring sound.
She gasped and groaned, she hoped and prayed,
But never left the ground.

One fateful day, the Pigglejay
Went down to Beachy Head.
"If I can't learn to fly", she sobbed,
"I'd just as soon be dead."

She jumped, and plummeted like lead,
A pinkish blur of motion,
But since, by chance, the tide was in,
She landed in the ocean.

And now she spends delightful days
With cuttlefish and kippers,
For what she thought were useless wings
Work perfectly as flippers.

The Quembling

The Quembling longed to have a friend
Who'd treat her with affection,
But every shy attempt would end
In laughter and rejection.

The others never ceased to mock
Her lumpy ears and toes,
Her straw-filled sleeves, her ragged frock,
Her bulbous turnip-nose.

And so she came to Earth to find
A friend to share her life,
A gentle soul, polite and kind,
Who'd take her for his wife.

She looked for him throughout the land
In village and in city,
Yet no one asked her for her hand,
Or even thought her pretty.

She traipsed through countryside and wood
Until, one moonlit night,
She cried with joy, for there he stood,
Her longed-for Mr Right.

She snuggled up, no longer shy,
And kissed him on the cheek,
Which brought a glimmer to his eye
Although he couldn't speak.

So there they stand, as in a dream;
Contentedly, she knows
That they've become a perfect team
For scaring off the crows.

The Rumpkin

The Rumpkin fell from outer space.
He hadn't meant to come;
He toppled from an asteroid—
He'd tripped on chewing-gum—
Then tumbled through the atmosphere
And landed on his bum.

He headed to Chicago
At the time of prohibition.
It seemed a likely city
For a fellow with ambition,
So he applied to Al Capone,
Who offered a position.

"Here's what ya gonna do", said Al.
"I need a new enforcer."
He paused to take a swig of hooch,
And slurped it from a saucer.
"The previous one was too polite—
I wanna guy who's coarser.

Defaulters get a warning shot;
Just knock 'em for a loop.
The second time, ya break their knees,
Or turn their brains to soup.
The third offense? An acid bath,
With nothing left but gloop.

But here's the thing—to get the job,
Ya gotta pass a test.
What's two plus two?" The Rumpkin frowned,
Then hesitantly guessed:
"Could it be three?" Capone just growled:
"Get lost, ya dopey pest!"

The Rumpkin took it equably;
He never held a grudge.
He looked for work at City Hall,
But no one there would budge.
Too stupid even for a cop,
He ended up a judge.

The Snidgit

I hardly dare mention the Snidgit;
He's such an unsavoury beast.
He will pick at his nose with his feculent toes,
And consider the contents a feast.

If he's bored, he will wriggle and fidget;
At dinner, he belches and farts.
When confronted with culture, he gawps like a vulture,
He couldn't care less for the arts.

His manners are frankly appalling;
In shops, he refuses to queue.
He'll poke with his brolly or shove with his trolley
To get to the till before you.

And if charity workers come calling
For aid for the sick and the poor,
"Do you think I am barmy? The Salvation Army?"
He'll tell them, and slam his front door.

He scratches his privates in public,
And sniffs at his armpits with glee.
He's pimply and podgy, he's dirty and dodgy—
How different from you and from me!

The Trilph

The Trilph is a delicate creature;
He's less than the size of a flea,
Yet he's perfectly formed; every feature
As handsome as handsome can be.

He worked in a travelling circus;
He trained all the acrobat fleas.
With a crack of his whip, they would hop and they'd skip,
And they'd even cavort on their knees.

There was one that he loved to distraction -
The ringmaster's daughter, no less.
On the flying trapeze, she was queen of the fleas,
But the Trilph was too shy to confess.

One evening, there came a disaster:
The maintenance fleas were on strike,
So they'd called in some ticks, who omitted to fix
The trapeze that was hung from a spike.

The ropes that supported her crumbled;
The crowd were all holding their breath;
The structure gave way, and she tumbled
To what would have been certain death.

But he ran to the spot, and he caught her;
She literally fell in his arms!
He eloped with the ringmaster's daughter;
They'd fallen for each other's charms.

Their children were small but athletic;
A tumbler, a juggler, a clown.
And so they decided, though sceptics derided,
To bring their own circus to town.

At last, they were ready to open;
The banner was proudly unfurled
"See the miniature fleas riding bareback on bees -
It's the tiniest show in the world!"

But time runs away like a robber ...
The words on her gravestone are these:
"In death as in life, my adorable wife,
And the queen of the flying trapeze."

The Urbloid

The Urbloid is a funny shape;
He's neither round nor square.
His head is like a rhomboid grape
With equilateral hair.

His eyelids are triangular,
His ears octagonal,
His nostrils are rectangular,
His mouth hexagonal.

His little legs are shaped like cones
On pyramidic feet,
With long, hypotenusal bones,
Euclideanly neat.

His body is, from neck to arse,
A parallelogram.
So take him when you go to class;
No need to swot and cram.
He's everything you need to pass
Your geometry exam.

For letter 'V', there seems to be
No other-worldly beast.
To compensate, I shall relate—

The Vegetable Feast

Asparagus and Broccoli detested one another,
Which made young Carrot rather sad; he loved them like a brother.
Hoping to reconcile the pair, he organized a party,
Inviting vegetable friends, and leafy litterati.

The first one to arrive was Dill, then Endive, Fennel, Garlic,
Herb, Iceberg Lettuce, Jersey Royal, Kale, and Leek from Harlech,
Then Mushroom, Nutmeg, Onion, Parsnip, Quince, Radicchio, Swede.
The Turnips came in evening dress, a handsome pair indeed.

The house was full to bursting point, no room for any more;
Though guests continued to arrive, they couldn't pass the door.
The U- to Y-'s were turned away, resentful and upset,
But sly Zucchini crashed the gate by posing as Courgette.

The younger sprouts were full of beans, and though the crowd was dense,
They blithely started playing squash, which gingered up events.
The music was provided by a band called "Sugar Beat"
Till someone let a rocket off, which knocked them off their feet.

"These kids have so much energy!" said Salsify to Spinach.
The revelry was clearly heard from Golders Green to Greenwich.
What rooty-tooty goings-on! What salad days! What capers!
The guests could hardly wait to read tomorrow's morning papers.

The party was a great success, the happy throng enraptured—
Until a giant hand appeared, and all of them were captured.
They lay upon the chopping board, a fearful, tearful group,
About to meet their destiny as vegetable soup.

The Wapsicles

The Wapsicles had dreamt of Earth,
A world where people ate and ate.
They sold their house for half its worth
And bought an interstellar jet.

They once were skinny creatures that
Could never get enough to eat,
But here, they've grown grotesquely fat,
And wobble on their bloated feet.

Though "Breakfast, Dinner, Lunch, and Tea
Are all a Wapsicle requires",
Or so they've heard, the family
Eats round the clock, and never tires

Of buns and burgers, snicks and snacks,
And greasy doughnuts that they dunk;
Their bulging freezer never lacks
A cornucopia of junk.

They stuff themselves with fat and grease,
With puddings, lollies, popsicles.
They're all so horribly obese
That neighbours call them "Dropsicals".

*****

Their lives were short, their coffins wide,
But they'd enjoyed their final fling.
The happy Wapsicles had died
From eating simply everything.

The Xenolith

I

The Xenolith is not a myth,
Though sceptics would deny it.
He's largely made of ancient stone
Resulting from his diet.

A million million years ago
He landed on this planet,
And found himself embedded in
A massive block of granite.

He lived a sedentary life,
Imprisoned in the rocks.
He didn't mind, although he wished
That he could change his socks.

II

But hunger and thirst overcame him;
He started to nibble the strata.
The granite - delicious, and highly nutritious -
Was merely a succulent starter.

Then layers of limestone and sandstone;
He cheerfully munched in the gloom.
Millennia passed till the day came, at last,
That he'd eaten a sizeable room.

In order to travel more freely,
He chewed out a series of tunnels
Both airy and bright, for he captured the light
Through an intricate system of funnels.

He invited his friends to a party,
Though reaching his place would take ages:
To get to his home, they must crunch through the tome
Of geology's petrified pages.

At last, all the guests were assembled;
The cavern was full chock-a-block;
The dance-floor was cramped as they stomped and they stamped
To 'The Old Carboniferous Rock'.

(As geologists will tell you, a xenolith is a rock fragment foreign to the rock in which it is embedded.)

The Yucketeer

Beware the smarmy Yucketeer,
Beware his oily greeting.
Remember that his mission here
Is lying, stealing, cheating.

He's from a planet in the Lyre,
Though he will say 'Orion'.
In every profitable fire
He has a crooked iron.

A master of the three-card trick,
A swindler without peer;
You will regret the day you met
The crafty Yucketeer.

He'll stop to greet you in the street
And ask you how it goes.
Before he leaves, you'd better count
Your fingers and your toes.

Oh, he's a sly one, he's a con;
He'll offer you a beer,
But when the bill arrives, he's gone,
The cunning Yucketeer.

Although he claims he's only come
To spend a brief vacation,
He's really here to "disappear"
The treasures of the nation.

He's twice as cool as any fridge;
He'll pocket Brighton Pier,
St Paul's Cathedral, London Bridge—
Beware the Yucketeer!

The Zoff

There's nothing much of interest to tell about the Zoff.
Though those who claim to know him say he dresses like a toff,
Especially when playing golf (that he pronounces 'goff'),
And sports a splendid lavender top-hat to don and doff,
While others say he smokes too much, which causes him to cough,
And keeps a crystal goblet for the wine he loves to quaff,
Yet snuffles up his dinner from a filthy wooden trough.
Regrettably, at all such groundless rumours I must scoff,
For no one's ever managed to set eyes upon the Zoff—
If they so much as glimpse his shadow, in a trice he's off!

Postlude

The Ayterzedd had paused for breath;
I told him we must run.
"Don't go!" he begged, "There's so much more;
I've scarcely yet begun:

Astrology, Biology,
Cosmology, Dontology,
Ecology, Fetology,
Geology, Histology,
Immunohematology,
(Just wait, I need to sneeze—atchee!
that's better!) Kremlinology,
Lithology, Mythology,
Neuroendocrinology,
Oenology, Psychology,
Quercology, Rheology,
Scatology, Theology,
Ufology, Virology,
(With my sincere apology,
there is no X-Y-ology),
and finally, Zoology."

"How kind", I said, "But we are pressed;
We must be on our way.
Of course, we'd love to hear the rest—
Perhaps another day ..."

About the Author

Brian Allgar was born in 1943, a mere 22 months before Hitler committed suicide, although no causal connection between the two events has ever been established.

Educated at Christ's Hospital, Horsham, and University College, Oxford, he joined the Civil Service where he vegetated for nine years. To the astonishment of his colleagues, he resigned in order to become a freelance computer software writer, a job that has taken him to France, Holland, Sweden, Italy, and the United States.

Although immutably English, he has lived in Paris since 1982. He started entering humorous competitions in 1967, but took a 35-year break, finally re-emerging in 2011 as a kind of Rip Van Winkle of the literary competition world.

His work has appeared in *The New Statesman, The Oldie, The Spectator, Flash500, Light Poetry, Lighten Up Online, Snakeskin, The Quarterly Review, The Great American Wise Ass Anthology, Measure, The Penguin Book of Limericks,* and possibly a few other places that he's forgottten. He also drinks malt whisky and writes music, which may explain his fondness for Mendelssohn's Scottish Symphony.

www.ingramcontent.com/pod-product-compliance
Lightning Source LLC
LaVergne TN
LVHW021626080426
835510LV00019B/2776